Y0-CJD-026

Fun with Abby & Alyssa ™

An Introduction to Sign Language

A day with Colors

Written by Grandpa Don
Illustrated by Liam Gooley

Written by Grandpa Don
Illustrated by Liam Gooley

Fun With Abby and Alyssa
A day with Colors
Copyright @ 2011 by DVM Consulting LLC

Illustrations Copyright @ 2011 by DVM Consulting
LLC

All rights reserved. This book may not be reproduced,
transmitted or stored in whole or in part by any
means, including graphic, electronic, or mechanical
without the express written consent of DVM
Consulting LLC except in the case of brief quotations
embodied in critical articles and reviews.

ISBN#: 978-0-9833163-1-2

Dedication

Abby and Alyssa are real people. They both have significant medical challenges and use sign language to talk. As growing sisters, their energy and charisma can be inspirational to anyone that wishes to learn.

This series of books is dedicated to Abby and Alyssa who inspire me, and to Grandma Gina who lives on within our hearts.

Grandpa Don

Hi! My name is
Abby and this is
my sister Alyssa.

Alyssa uses signs
instead of words to
talk. She makes these
signs with her hands.

You already know some signs like waving your hand to say hi.

Come with us today and we'll learn more signs for colors!

Hi: Open hand waved side to side.

Today we're going
to learn the signs
for different
colors..

Let's see what colors
we can find and
sign them together!

Colors: Wiggle the fingers of the right "5" hand in front of the mouth.

What color is the fire truck?

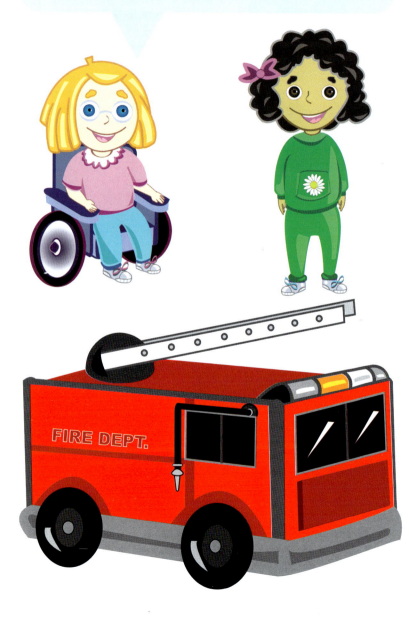

The Sign: Brush lower lip with tip of right index finger and repeat.

Let's all make the sign for red!

Red: Brush lower lip with tip of right index finger and repeat.

What color is the ball?

The Sign: **Right hand making "B" sign, palm moving left, wave back and forth.**

That's right, the ball is blue!

Let's all make the sign for blue!

Blue: Right hand making "B" sign, palm moving left, wave back and forth.

What color are the blocks?

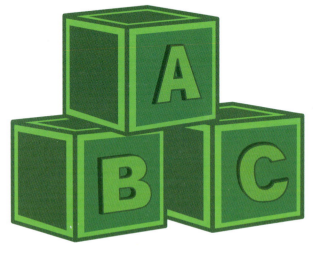

The Sign: Right hand making "G" sign, shake back and forth.

That's right, the blocks are green!

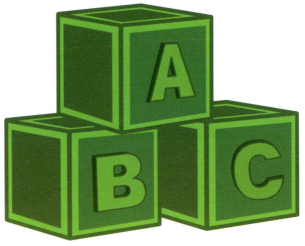

Let's all make the sign for green!

Green: Right hand making "G" sign, shake back and forth.

What color are the shovel and pail?

The Sign: Right hand making "C" sign, with the palm facing left, place at mouth and squeeze into an "S" sign and repeat.

That's right, the shovel and pail are orange!

Let's all make the sign for orange!

Orange: Right hand making "C" sign, with the palm facing left, place at mouth and squeeze into an "S" sign and repeat.

What color is the kite?

The Sign: Draw right index finger across forehead from left to right.

That's right, the kite is black!

Let's all make the sign for black!

Black: Draw right index finger across forehead from left to right.

What color is the snowman?

The Sign: Fingertips of right "5" hand on chest, palm facing in, pull hand forward into "O" sign.

That's right, the snowman is white!

Let's all make the sign for white!

White: Fingertips of right "5" hand on chest, palm facing in, pull hand forward into "O" sign.

The Sign: Slide index finger of right hand making "B" sign, palm facing left, down the right cheek.

That's right, the teddy bear is brown!

Let's all make the sign for brown!

Brown: Slide index finger of right hand making "B" sign, palm facing left, down the right cheek.

What color is the doll's dress?

The Sign: Right hand making the "P" sign, shake back and forth from the wrist.

That's right, the doll's dress is purple!

Let's all make the sign for purple!

Purple: Right hand making the "P" sign, shake back and forth from the wrist.

We've learned the signs for many colors today.

It's time for Alyssa and me to go home...

Let's all make the sign for good-bye!

Good-Bye: Wave open hand up and down.

For more fun with sign language, you can practice your A,B,C's and numbers!

alphabet

A

B

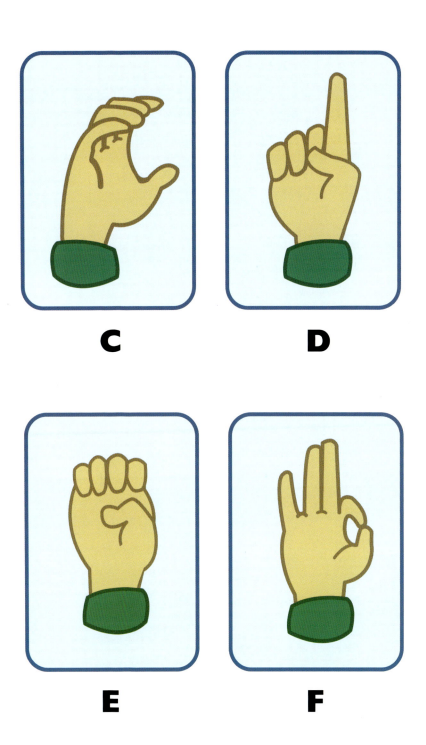

C

D

E

F

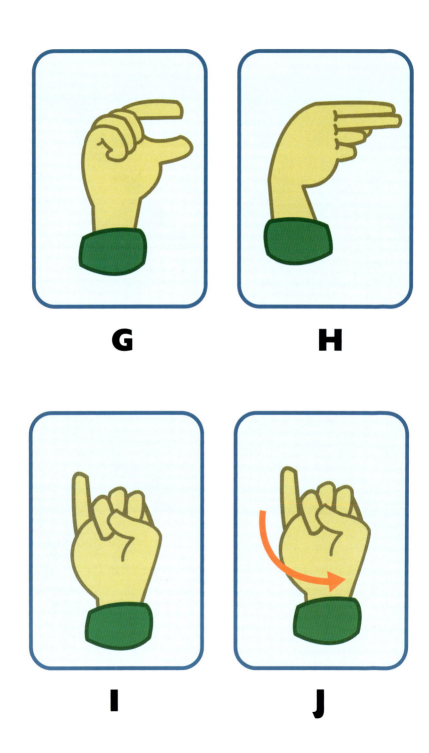

G

H

I

J

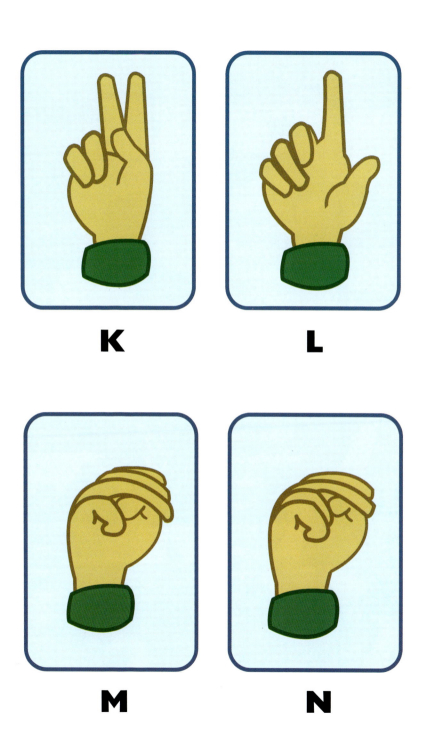

K

L

M

N

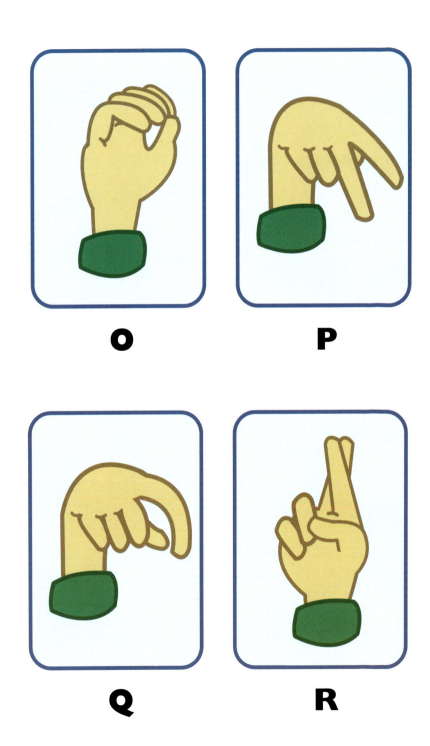

O

P

Q

R

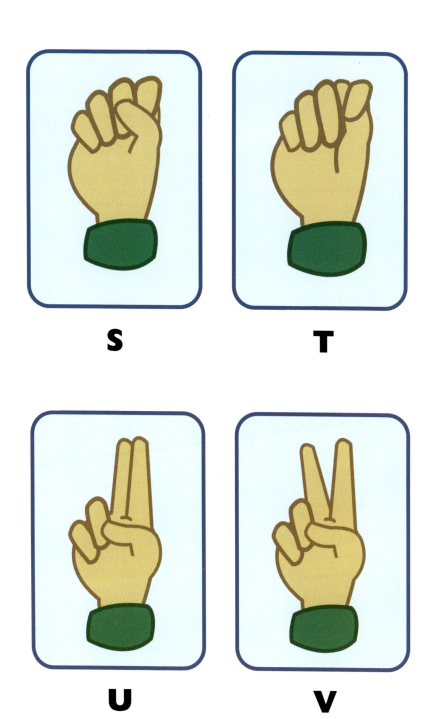

S

T

U

V

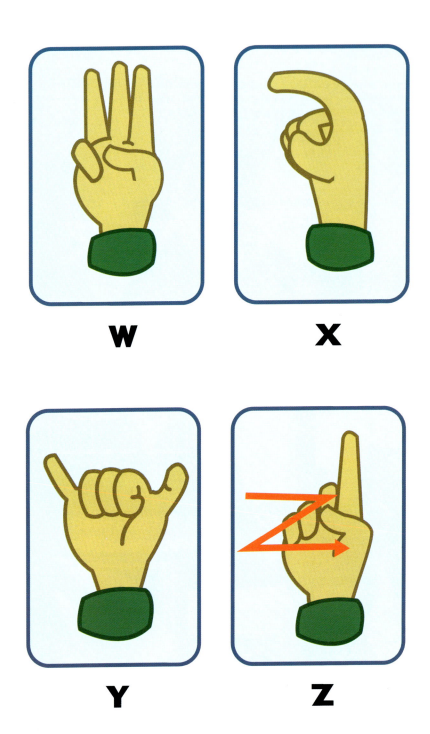

W　　**X**

Y　　**Z**

numbers 1 - 10

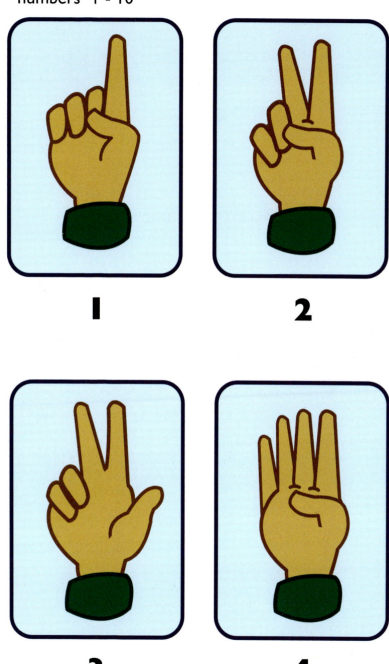

1

2

3

4

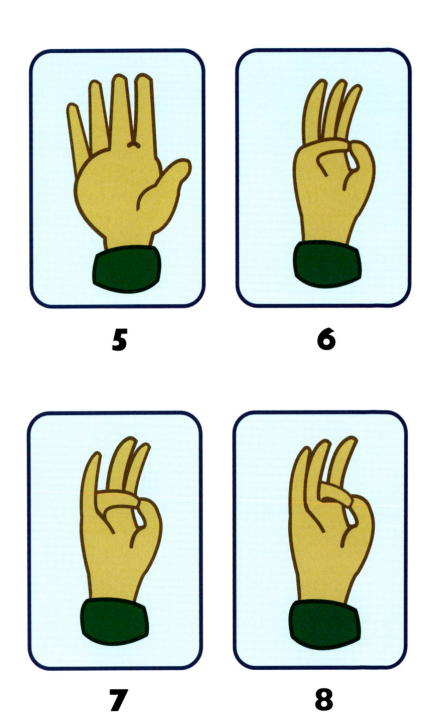

5

6

7

8

9

10

Acknowledgements

Some words in sign language have multiple acceptable signs. In those instances where multiple signs were available, Grandpa Don chose the sign most appropriate for Abby and Alyssa.

Grandpa Don encourages readers who want to learn more about sign language to read:

- "The Art of Sign Language" by
  Christopher Brown; Random House.

- "Webster's Unabridged American
  Sign Language Dictionary" by Elaine Costello, PHD.

And to also visit these websites:

- www.signingsavvy.com

- www.lessontutor.com